WITHDRAWN

Artisans Around the World

Southwest Pacific

Sharon Franklin, Rhonda Krafchin, and Cynthia A. Black

RSVP

RAINTREE
STECK-VAUGHN
PUBLISHERS
A Steck-Vaughn Company

Austin, Texas

www.steck-vaughn.com

Developed by Franklin Tull, Inc.,
Manager: Sharon Franklin
Designer: Dahna Solar
Maps: Terragraphics, Inc.
Illustrators: Dahna Solar and James Cloutier
Picture Researcher: Mary Tull
Projects: Cynthia A. Black

Raintree Steck-Vaughn Publishers Staff
Project Manager: Joyce Spicer
Editor: Pam Wells
Electronic Production: Scott Melcer

Photo Credits: Don Eastman/The Stock Solution: pp. 8UL, 8UR, 11UR; Robert Holmes: p. 8LL; David Frazier/The Stock Solution: p. 8LR; CORBIS/Ales Fevzer: p. 9LR; Peggy Grove: pp. 10CL, 12L, 13UR, 13UL; Carl Purcell/The Stock Solution: p. 12UR; "Warntaparri" by Janet Long Nakamarra/http://www.wr.com.au/jinart/gallery.htm: p. 14L; CORBIS/Ralph A. Clevenger: p. 13LR; CORBIS: p. 18LL; CORBIS/Arne Hodalic: p. 18UL; CORBIS/Michael S. Yamashito: p. 18UR; CORBIS/Wolfgang Kaehler: pp. 18LR, 20UR, 21LR, 40UR; CORBIS/Yann Arthus Bertrand: p. 19LR; CORBIS/Wayne Lawler: p. 21UL; CORBIS/Danny Lehman: p. 22LR; Courtesy of New Zealand Tourism Board: pp. 26UL, 26UR, 26CL, 26LR, 27UR, 28UR, 30CL, 31UL, 32UR, 32L; CORBIS/E.O. Hoppé: p. 29LR; CORBIS/Werner Forman: p. 30UR; CORBIS/Matthew McKee, Eye Ubiquitous: p. 31LR; CORBIS/Bill Ross: p. 36UL; CHOICE Humanitarian: pp. 36UR, 38UL; Lea Ann King: pp. 36LL, 39LL; CORBIS: p. 37UR. All project photos by James Cloutier.
[**Photo credit key:** First Letter: U-Upper; C-Center, L-Lower; Second letter: R-Right; L-Left]

Library of Congress Cataloging-in-Publication Data
Franklin, Sharon.
Southwest Pacific / Sharon Franklin, Rhonda Krafchin, and Cynthia A. Black.
p. cm. — (Artisans around the world)
Includes bibliographical references and index.
Summary: Presents brief historical information about the Southwest Pacific as well as descriptions of the cultures of the people and instructions for making craft projects representative of them.
ISBN 0-7398-0120-1
1. Art, Australian aboriginal — Juvenile literature. 2. Art, Maori—Juvenile literature. 3. Art, Pacific Island — Juvenile literature. 4. Ethnic art — Oceania — Juvenile literature. 5. Artisans — Oceania — Juvenile literature. 6. Creative activities and seat work—Juvenile literature. [1. Art, Australian aboriginal. 2. Art, Maori. 3. Art, Pacific Island. 4. Artisans. 5. Handicraft.] I. Krafchin, Rhonda. II. Black, Cynthia A. III. Title. IV. Series.
GN666.F72 1999
306'.099—dc21
98-53098
CIP AC

Printed and bound in the United States
1 2 3 4 5 6 7 8 9 0 WO 03 02 01 00 99

Table of Contents

The icons next to the projects in the Table of Contents identify the easiest and the most challenging project in the book. This may help you decide which project to do first.

⇨ easiest project

✪ most challenging project

INDONESIA

PAPUA
NEW
GUINEA

AUSTRALIA

NEW
ZEALAND

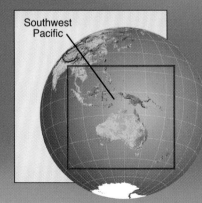

Southwest
Pacific

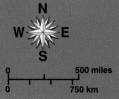

N
W   E
S

0   500 miles
0   750 km

Introduction to Artisans Around the World

There are many ways to learn about the history and present-day life of people in other countries. In school, students often study the history of a country to learn about its people. In this series, you will learn about the history, geography, and the way of life of groups of people through their folk art. People who create folk art are called **artisans.** They are skilled in an art, a craft, or a trade. You will then have a chance to create your own folk art, using your own ideas and symbols.

What Is Folk Art?

Folk art is not considered "fine art." Unlike many fine artists, folk artisans do not generally go to school to learn how to do their art. Very few folk artists are known as "famous" outside of their countries or even their towns. Folk art is the art of everyday people of a region. In this series, folk art also includes primitive art, that is, the art of the first people to be in an area. But, beware! Do not let this fool you into thinking that folk art is not "real" art. As you will see, the quality of the folk art in this series is amazing by any standards.

Folk art comes from the heart and soul of common people. It is an expression of their feelings. Often, it shows their personal, political, or religious beliefs. It may also have a practical purpose or meet a specific need, such as the need for shelter. In many cases, the folk art in the "Artisans Around the World" series comes from groups of people who did not even have a word for art in their culture. Art was simply what people did. It was a part of being human.

Introduction to *Southwest Pacific*

In this book, you will learn about these crafts and the people who do them:

X-ray painting in Australia

Carved wood shields in Papua New Guinea

Taaniko weaving in New Zealand

Batik in Indonesia

Then you will learn how to do projects of your own.

Here are some questions to think about as you read this book:

Which of these folk arts helped to meet people's needs?
Which ones helped people meet their basic needs?

Which folk arts expressed people's religious, political, or personal views?

Were some of these folk arts traditionally created mostly by men or by women?
Why do you think that was so? Is it still true today?

How did the history of a country influence some folk art traditions?

How did the geography, including the natural resources, of a country
influence some folk art traditions? How did people get folk art materials
that they needed but that were not found in their region?

Do some folk art traditions tell a story about a group of people or a culture?
If so, in what way?

How have these folk art traditions been passed down from generation to generation?

Folk Art Today

Reading about these folk art traditions, as well as creating your own folk art,
will increase your respect for the people who first did them.
Do you think some of these art forms, such as carved wood shields, could be created
faster or more easily using machines, like power saws, or technology, like the computer?
Do you think anything would be lost by doing so, even if it were possible?

All of these folk art traditions of the Southwest Pacific began long ago.
Can you think of any new folk art traditions being started now, in the
United States or in other countries? If so, what are they?
If not, why do you think there are no new traditions?

Safety Guidelines

These folk art projects are a lot of fun to do, but it's important to follow basic safety rules as you work. Here are some guidelines to help as you complete the projects in this book. Work slowly and carefully. That way you can enjoy the process.

1. Part of being a responsible person of any age is knowing when to ask for help. Some of these projects are challenging. Ask an adult for help whenever you need it. Even where the book does not tell you to, feel free to ask for help if you need it.

2. Handle all pointed tools, such as scissors, in a safe manner. Keep them stored in a safe place when not in use.

3. When painting, protect your clothing with an old shirt or a smock. When wet, acrylic paint can be removed with water. After it dries, it cannot be removed.

4. Woodworking Safety
   • You must have an adult work with you.
   • Learn the correct way to use a tool, and use it for its intended purpose only.
   • Always clamp the wood to a stable base before carving.
   • Use common sense! Never put your fingers in front of the chisel when you are carving.
   • Cut away from yourself and others.

5. Wax Safety
   • You must have an adult work with you.
   • Tie your hair back and roll up your sleeves.
   • Move slowly and carefully when working near hot wax.
   • Keep the temperature of the wax below 300° F (150° C). Above this temperature, the wax will begin to smoke and could ignite into flames.
   • Never leave the wax unattended when it is heating.
   • If the wax should catch on fire, use a pan lid or towel to smother the flames. Never pour water on it. Have a fire extinguisher nearby, just in case.

6. Dye Safety
   • Ask an adult to mix the dyes for you and to work with you on the dyeing.
   • Dyes will stain clothes, tables, floors, and skin. Cover every surface with plastic. Wear an apron to protect your clothes. Wear rubber gloves to protect your hands.
   • Don't use the dye tub or mixing containers for food. Thoroughly wash dye out of the sink.

By the way, part of being an artist involves cleaning up! Be sure to clean up your work area when you are finished. Also, remember to thank anyone who helped you.

The Olgas, a group of rocks in Australia's Northern Territory, may be more than three billion years old.

PACIFIC OCEAN

INDONESIA

PAPUA NEW GUINEA

The Great Barrier Reef stretches for 1,250 miles (2,010 km) along the north-west coast. It contains more than 400 kinds of coral and 1,500 species of fish.

TIMOR SEA

Maningrida

Darwin ○

Western Arnhem Land

Gulf of Carpentaria

CORAL SEA

INDIAN OCEAN

NORTHERN TERRITORY

AUSTRALIA

Great Barrier Reef

Eastern Highlands

Great Sandy Desert

G r e a t   W e s t e r n

Yuendumu ○

Papunya ○

Gibson Desert

Alice ○ Springs

P l a t e a u

▲ Uluru (Ayers Rock)

Central Lowlands

QUEENSLAND

Ernabella ○

Simpson Desert

Great Victoria Desert

WESTERN AUSTRALIA

Coober ○ Pedy

Lake Eyre

SOUTH AUSTRALIA

Brisbane ○

○ Perth

Great Australian Bight

Darling River

NEW SOUTH WALES

Adelaide ○

Murray River

○ Sydney

☆ **Canberra**

VICTORIA

Mt. Kosciusko ▲

Melbourne ○

TASMAN SEA

Koala bears are one of many animals that are unique to Australia.

Sydney, with its modern Opera House, is one of Australia's largest cities.

TASMANIA

N W E S

| 0 | | 500 miles |
| 0 | | 750 km |

Australia

The Land Down Under

Australia, the land "down under," lies within the Southern Hemisphere. In fact, Australia comes from the Latin word *australis*, or southern. The mainland includes five states—Western Australia, South Australia, Queensland, New South Wales, and Victoria—and an area called the Northern Territory. The sixth state, Tasmania, is an island off the southeast coast.

Australia is an island continent, but long ago it was not an island at all. Some geologists believe Australia was once connected to South America, Africa, and Antarctica. At one time in its long history, it may also have been connected to Asia by a giant land bridge.

The First Australians

The first Australians were the Aborigines. No one knows exactly when or how they came to be in Australia. The oldest remains found up to now place them in Australia for more than 60,000 years. Some people believe the Aborigines came across a land bridge from Asia. The Aborigines disagree. According to their history, they were in Australia from the beginning.

Today, Australia's big cities are a mix of people from many different places. Many Aborigines, however, live outside the big cities in the rural areas of Australia. Regardless of where they live, Aborigines share a common identity as the first Australians and a growing pride in their heritage. Their traditional culture, one of the most unusual and ancient in the world, includes a highly developed artistic tradition that connects them to their ancestors. Although Aboriginal stories and beliefs go back thousands of years, it is not a culture that is fixed in the past. Aborigines have shown a remarkable ability to change and endure for a very, very long time.

Aboriginal athlete Cathy Freeman ▶ proudly celebrates victory.

Australia Facts

Name: Australia (Commonwealth of Australia), "Down Under"
Capital: Canberra
Nearest neighbors: Indonesia, Papua New Guinea, Solomon Islands, New Caledonia, Fiji, and New Zealand
Oceans: Lies between the Indian and South Pacific oceans
Population: 18 million total; Aborigine population about 250,000
Language: Official language: English; once there were more than 250 Aboriginal languages; today, only around 30 are taught to children and spoken on a regular basis
Size: 2,966,150 sq. mi. (7,682,328 sq km)
High/Low Points: Mount Kosciusko, 7,310 ft. (2,228 m); Lake Eyre, about 40 ft. (12 m) below sea level
Climate: The driest continent after Antarctica; the north has heavy monsoon rains in the summer and occasional tropical cyclones; the south receives most rainfall in winter; temperatures range from over 104° F (40° C) in summer to 45° F (7° C) in winter; seasons opposite those in the Northern Hemisphere, because it lies south of the equator
Wildlife: Emus, koalas, red kangaroos, platypuses, dingos, Tasmanian devils, wombats, knobtail geckos, frilled lizards; many species unique to Australia; 700 species of native birds, including the world's only black swans
Plants: Over 600 species of wattle (acacias); 500 species of eucalyptus (gum) trees; many species of plants native only to Australia

Aboriginal Life Before 1788

When the first white settlers arrived from Britain in 1788, about 500 Aboriginal tribes, each with its own language, social system, and territory, were already living there. An estimated 750,000 people lived mostly on the north and east coasts and in the Murray River Valley. Four thousand Aborigines also lived on the island of Tasmania.

The Aborigines had lived in harmony with their harsh environment for many thousands of years. They were nomadic hunters and gatherers who had created a stable and efficient way of life. They communicated through music, song, spoken literature, and their art. Family relationships were extremely important. Family groups, or clans, lived together on certain lands and performed their own rituals. Sharing was very important. The Aborigines believed that to be human was to share.

▲ *Returning boomerangs* were used to kill birds and in traditional hunting games. *Non-returning boomerangs* were used for hunting and as weapons. They are heavier and are often beautifully decorated.

New Arrivals

For a time, the Aborigines offered to help the white settlers survive in the new land. But soon the settlers began forcing the Aborigines off their land, claiming it for their own. Thousands of Aborigines were tortured and killed. Many also died from diseases brought by the Europeans. The Aborigines had no **immunity,** or resistance to these diseases. Their spears and boomerangs, weapons created for hunting, were no match for the settlers' guns and horses. Those who survived were moved off their ancestral lands into **settlements.** By 1933, the Aborigines numbered less than 74,000.

▲ Early Aboriginal rock art.

What Is That?

When the English arrived, they saw many species of plants and animals they had never seen before. Since there was no English word for many of these strange-looking things, they called them by their Aboriginal names. Aboriginal words adapted by the English include *kangaroo, boomerang, dingo* (a wild dog), and *billabong* (a dry river that fills with water only after a heavy rain).

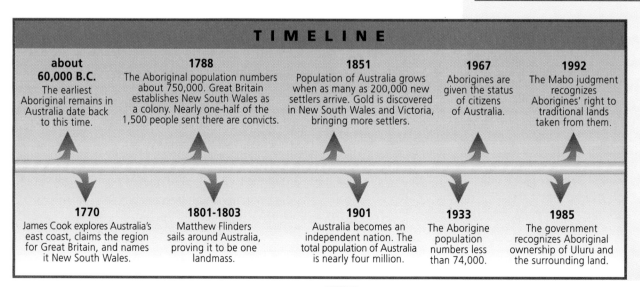

TIMELINE				
about 60,000 B.C. The earliest Aboriginal remains in Australia date back to this time.	**1788** The Aboriginal population numbers about 750,000. Great Britain establishes New South Wales as a colony. Nearly one-half of the 1,500 people sent there are convicts.	**1851** Population of Australia grows when as many as 200,000 new settlers arrive. Gold is discovered in New South Wales and Victoria, bringing more settlers.	**1967** Aborigines are given the status of citizens of Australia.	**1992** The Mabo judgment recognizes Aborigines' right to traditional lands taken from them.
1770 James Cook explores Australia's east coast, claims the region for Great Britain, and names it New South Wales.	**1801-1803** Matthew Flinders sails around Australia, proving it to be one landmass.	**1901** Australia becomes an independent nation. The total population of Australia is nearly four million.	**1933** The Aborigine population numbers less than 74,000.	**1985** The government recognizes Aboriginal ownership of Uluru and the surrounding land.

Great Western Plateau

The Great Western Plateau includes Western Australia, much of South Australia and the Northern Territory, and some of western Queensland. Most of the **plateau** is **outback,** Australia's dry, sparsely populated interior. There are many cattle and sheep ranches, some of which cover more than 1,000 square miles (2,600 sq km).

▲ Tourists go to Alice Springs to begin their exploration of Australia's remote outback and to see Uluru.

Alice Springs is called "the capital of the center." It is a popular starting place for tourists who want to see the outback. They can also visit Uluru (also called Ayers Rock), one of the world's largest rocks, or see the work of Aboriginal artists at the Papunya settlement. Farther south lies Lake Eyre, and beyond that the town of Coober Pedy. In Aboriginal language, Coober Pedy means "hole in the ground" or "white man's burrow." Almost all the buildings, including houses, stores, and even hotels, are below ground. Underground living protects residents from the searing desert heat.

The Central Lowlands and Eastern Highlands

The hot, dry Central Lowlands cover most of New South Wales and Queensland, and some of Victoria and South Australia. The Eastern Highlands area includes the coastal area of New South Wales and Queensland, much of Victoria, and Tasmania. This region has the highest mountains, more fertile soil, and more rain than other regions. Australia's two largest cities, Sydney and Melbourne, lie in the southern half of the highlands. Sydney was built over an area that the Aborigines of long ago were forced to leave. Now, the community of Redfern is bringing them back.

Redfern

Redfern is an Aboriginal community in the center of Sydney that began in the 1930s. Many Aboriginal poets, artists, and political leaders were attracted to the community in the 1970s. Today, Redfern runs its own schools, legal service, art galleries, and radio station. It is a vibrant community and a symbol of the strength and vision of Aboriginal people.

Lake Eyre

Dry lakes, called *playas,* are common in South Australia and Western Australia. These dry lake beds fill only after heavy rains. Lake Eyre, the lowest point on the continent, is a *playa.*

▲ Opal mining is Coober Pedy's biggest industry.

The Dreaming

The Aborigines are linked to the land and nature through Ancestral Beings who, according to Aboriginal belief, created the world. Aborigines call the time of creation Dreamtime, or the Dreaming. During this sacred time, Dreamtime Beings emerged from the underground and moved over the earth, singing. They sang all living things into existence. Where they emerged, the places they visited, where they stopped, and where they went back under the earth became the waterholes, rocks, rivers, and hills.

Re-enacting Dreamtime

Dreamtime explains the universe and defines the laws and guidelines by which Aborigines live. Aborigines help Dreamtime Beings by performing rituals, helping each other, and by caring for sacred sites. In exchange, the Dreamtime Beings help Aboriginal girls become women and boys become men. They increase the food supply and help the spirits of the dead.

▲ Aboriginal elders who are male pass on designs and their sacred meanings to young males.

Aboriginal Art

Most Aboriginal art is produced for religious purposes. Aboriginal art, rituals, songs, and dances often re-enact, or retell, important Dreamtime events and Beings. Symbolic designs may be drawn on bark, on rock, or on the ground. Some Aboriginal clans paint their bodies with feathers and **ochre,** an impure red or yellow iron ore found mainly in Western Australia.

There has to be a special connection between the Being, the artist, and the design being made. Both in the past and present, these designs contain many layers of knowledge. Elder males have the special responsibility and gift for passing on these designs to younger males. Elder females pass on sacred information to younger females. The elders decide when to introduce a design and explain its deeper meanings.

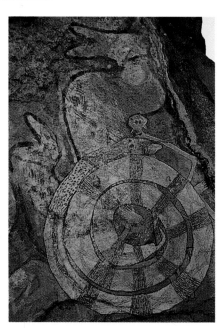

This Aboriginal design, called the ▶ Rainbow Serpent Dreamtime Being, contains a snake and a female figure.

Uluru

According to Aboriginal beliefs, Kuniya the carpet snake was an Ancestral Being who camped on a flat sand hill. The sand hill turned to stone and became Uluru. Today, this huge rock is a protected, sacred site, or place, of the Aborigines and the symbolic heart of the country.

▲ *Dilly* bag

▲ A fish created in the X-ray style

Bark Painting from Western Arnhem Land

Two styles of painting, the *Mimi* style and the X-ray style, originated in Western Arnhem Land in the northern part of Australia's Northern Territory. Both styles are seen in rock paintings. They are also painted on bark from eucalyptus and other trees. According to Aboriginal beliefs, *Mimi* spirits are thin, kindly Dreamtime spirits that live in the cracks of rocks. *Mimi* figures are painted as slender, sticklike figures in shades of red ochre against a plain background, so the figure will stand out. They are usually shown in action—dancing, running, or hunting.

X-ray style paintings feature many-colored images of birds, reptiles, fish, human beings, and spirit figures. Instead of painting just the "shell" of a figure, the internal structure, including the bones, heart, and other organs, is included. Some Aborigines say that revealing the inside is a way to show the object as living.

Ground Painting From Central Australia

Traditional ground painting began in the Western Desert Region of central Australia for use in ceremonies. Aboriginal artists sing as they create the art. It is said that they sing the art into existence. First, the ground is prepared with grooves and shallow trenches. Designs are added using feather down or a white puffy material from the kapok tree. Spirals, lines, circles, and points are used to show the coming out and disappearing of Dreamtime Beings. Traditionally, this form of art is not permanent. When the ceremony is over, the painting is erased.

Maningrida

Maningrida, a settlement in northern Australia, is known for its magnificent baskets woven by women. Weaving is one way women pass on their knowledge and display their artistry. The first Creator Being in this region was a woman who wore a *dilly* bag of woven fibers on her back. In this bag she carried all the children, plants, and animals who would populate Australia. Paintings on rock, bark, and canvas often recall this Dreamtime event.

This design is in the ▶ style of Western Desert ground painting.

Papunya Tula Artists Group

In 1959, the Australian government established Papunya, northwest of Alice Springs, as an Aboriginal settlement. The male elders from many clans who were forced to move there saw the need to bring back the Dreamtime stories and rituals, even in a place that was not their real home. They began to do ground painting again, recreating the beliefs of their old desert lifestyle. They painted in groups, away from other people. As they worked, they chanted the songs that told the stories of the designs.

In the 1970s, they were encouraged to make their designs permanent by painting them on board and canvas, using acrylic paints and brushes. The Papunya Tula Artists Group was formed. Their paintings, once seen only in a proper ritual context, are now owned by people all over the world. Dotted patterns are a part of this Western Desert painting style, along with the use of yellow and red ochre, black, and white.

▲ Almost any object can be decorated in the Western Desert painting style.

Looking to the Future

The designs painted on bodies or on the ground, on rock and on bark, as well as on canvas and watercolor paper, convey several layers of knowledge. There is the meaning that anyone can know, and there are deeper layers of meaning that are known only to male and female tribal members who are ready to understand them. There was a time when ground paintings and other religious art were only created and shown as a part of a religious ceremony, or ritual. Dreamings now are being created for all eyes to see. Art for public view can still record belief systems but may not include the deeper meanings. If they are included, these meanings will not be explained to the general public.

◄ Janet Long Nakamarra was born in 1960 in Warntaparri, the traditional land of her people. Her Aunt May and Aunt Molly Napurrula showed her how to paint the traditional body paint designs for her Warntaparri Dreaming. Her paintings tell about the myths and religion of her people. Nakamarra is becoming well known worldwide as an artist .

Women Painters

Both Aboriginal women and men have made important artistic contributions. They continue to pass on their beliefs and knowledge about the Dreamtime. Pitjantjatjara women artists from Ernabella began their painting tradition in the 1940s and 1950s. They also began the ground painting tradition at Yuendumu. One famous Aboriginal artist, Emily Kame Kngwarreye, came from the Utopia area in the Central Desert.

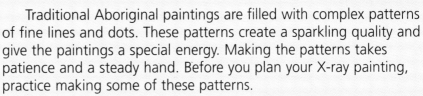

Tools

- drawing board
- paintbrushes
- pencil
- matchsticks

Materials

- watercolor paper
- tape
- acrylic paints (black, white, red oxide, yellow oxide)
- wax paper
- ruler (optional)
- paper
- transfer paper

Experiment with Painting

3. Mark off four sections on the watercolor paper.

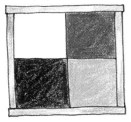

4. Paint thin rows of parallel lines.

5. Practice cross-hatching.

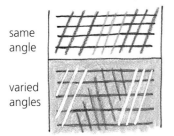

same angle

varied angles

Experiment with the patterns used by Aboriginal artists. Then create your own painting in the X-ray style.

Experiment with Painting

Traditional Aboriginal paintings are filled with complex patterns of fine lines and dots. These patterns create a sparkling quality and give the paintings a special energy. Making the patterns takes patience and a steady hand. Before you plan your X-ray painting, practice making some of these patterns.

1. Originally, Aboriginal artists painted on bark, on rock, and on the ground. Today, they also use paper, cardboard, and canvas. Watercolor paper will work well for this project. Tape a small piece of watercolor paper to a drawing board so it won't curl up.

2. The traditional colors used in X-ray paintings are red, yellow, white, and black. Read the Acrylic Paint Hints. Squeeze out a small amount of each color on a piece of wax paper. Dip a brush in water, and test the paint on the paper. It should be thick enough to cover well.

3. Divide the watercolor paper into four sections. Use a wide brush to paint each section with a different background color. Let the paint dry. *(See diagram.)*

4. *Cross-hatching* is a common feature of X-ray paintings. Use a very fine brush to paint rows of thin parallel lines. Space the lines as evenly as you can. If you want, you can draw light guidelines first with a pencil and ruler. *(See diagram.)*

5. Paint lines that cross the first lines. Make the cross lines all at the same angle, or vary the angles. Try alternating the colors of cross lines. Experiment with different color combinations. *(See diagram.)*

Acrylic Paint Hints

- Protect your clothing with an old shirt or a smock. When acrylic paint is still wet, it can be removed with water. When it dries, it cannot be removed.

- Acrylic paints dry quickly. Mix only a small amount of each color. If the paint begins to dry out, moisten it with a sprinkle of water.

- Never let paint dry in a brush. When you are finished painting, wash the brushes thoroughly with soap and water.

▲ Practice painting cross-hatches and dots.

6. Dots are sometimes used to fill shapes in X-ray paintings but are used more often in Western Desert style paintings. Use a matchstick to apply the dots. You can paint the dots in orderly rows or not. *(See diagram.)*

6. Use dots to fill shapes.

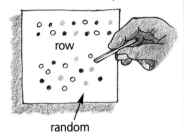

row

random

7. Dots are often applied inside bars that separate sections of cross-hatching. *(See diagram.)*

7. Apply dots inside bars.

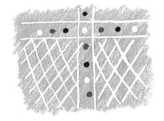

Plan an X-ray Painting

Aboriginal paintings have many layers of meaning. They tell the stories of the Dreaming. The figures and shapes are symbols of the Dreamtime Beings. They may also show places the Dreamtime Beings visited that have become Australian landmarks, such as Uluru (Ayers Rock). Every mark has a message.

1. To plan your own painting, think of a story or message that is meaningful to you. Decide on the images you will use. You may want to choose animals, people, objects, or landmarks, such as rocks or water. Geometric shapes, such as circles and diamonds, are common and can have many meanings. Read the hints on this page.

2. Plan the layout on a large piece of paper. Sometimes the page is divided into sections with dotted bars. Each section represents an event in the story or an area of the land. *(See diagram.)*

Plan an X-ray Painting

2. Plan the layout.

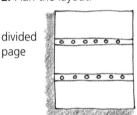

divided page

3. Draw the outlines.

Helpful Hints

■ Circles often stand for important landmarks, such as waterholes and camps.

■ Dotted bars may symbolize underground waterways or the tracks of Dreamtime Beings.

■ Diamonds sometimes stand for the cells in a beehive.

3. Draw the outlines of the images. Show only the basic parts. Draw animal figures from the angle that best shows the animal's important features. *(See diagram.)*

4. X-ray style paintings show the anatomy, or body structure, of animals and people. This style is sometimes thought to be a metaphor for the living landscape. Draw some parts of the skeleton, such as the backbone and the ribs. *(See diagram.)*

top view

side view

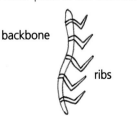

4. Draw parts of the skeleton.

backbone

ribs

5. Draw joints and eyes.

joints   eyes

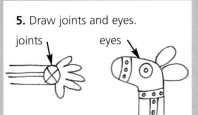

6. Draw simple organs.

heart and lungs

liver

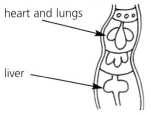

7. Plan where you will add patterns.

background

inside of image

Make an X-ray Painting

2. Trace over the main outlines.

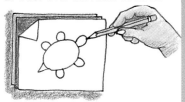

3. Paint the inside of the images.

These X-ray paintings by ▶
students each tell a story.

---

5. Use lines, dotted bands, or circles to show divisions at the joints of the neck, shoulders, hips, ankles, etc. Also draw the eyes. *(See diagram.)*

6. Some animals are shown with simple shapes of organs. Research animal anatomies for the correct locations of organs, such as the heart and lungs. *(See diagram.)*

7. Plan where you will add cross-hatching and other patterns. You can fill areas of the background with patterns. You can also divide areas inside the images with dotted bands and fill these areas with patterns. Leave some areas a solid color for variety. *(See diagram.)*

Make an X-ray Painting

1. Tape down a new piece of watercolor paper and paint the background color. Red is the most common color. Let it dry.

2. Place a piece of transfer paper on the watercolor paper with your X-ray plan on top. To transfer the design, trace over the main outlines of the figures and shapes with a pencil. *(See diagram.)*

3. Paint the inside of the images with solid colors that contrast with the background. Emphasize the most important shapes with bolder colors. Dry again. *(See diagram.)*

4. Begin to add the details and patterns. Take your time and do a careful job. Continue to add layers of detail and color until the painting sparkles with energy.

5. When your painting is dry, mount it on mat board.

Helpful Hints

■ Cross-hatching may indicate skin, scales, feathers. It may also indicate rocks, sand, grasses, or swamps.

■ In the Western Desert style, dots may indicate rain, fire, or clouds.

■ Changes in the colors of patterns may indicate a change in landscape.

PACIFIC OCEAN

Papua New Guinea's mangrove swamps are home to a wide variety of animals, plants, and insects.

Feathers from the bird of paradise are highly prized. This bird is pictured on the national flag.

Admiralty Islands

Bismarck Archipelago

New Ireland

BISMARCK SEA

IRIAN JAYA

Sepik River

PAPUA NEW GUINEA

Mt. Wilhelm ▲

Rabaul ○

New Britain

Bougainville

SOLOMON SEA

Fly River

Gulf of Papua

Port Moresby ☆

Torres Strait

Milne Bay

Young women in Papua New Guinea learn how to do chores, care for animals and children, and grow a garden.

CORAL SEA

Storyboards are used to tell traditional stories and to teach tribal history.

N
W ✴ E
S

| 0 | | 200 miles |
| 0 | | 250 km |

AUSTRALIA

Papua New Guinea

Papua New Guinea Facts

Name: Papua New Guinea
Capital: Port Moresby
Nearest Neighbors: Irian Jaya, Indonesia (Western half of New Guinea island); Australia; Solomon Islands
Population: Over 4 million; nearly all are Melanesians
Language: Official language: English; Tok Pisin (Pidgin English), Motu, and over 700 other distinct native languages
Size: 178,704 sq. mi. (462,840 sq km); Mainland Papua New Guinea is located on New Guinea, the second largest island in the world
High/Low Points: Mount Wilhelm 14,762 ft. (4,498 m); sea level
Climate: Most of the lowlands generally hot and humid, with temperatures around 86-90° F (30-32° C); higher elevation temperatures around 72° F (22° C); dry savanna around Port Moresby; constant threat of earthquakes and volcanoes in this Pacific Ocean region known as the Ring of Fire
Wildlife: Over 700 bird species, 250 mammals, over 200 reptiles; coral reefs, fish, birds of paradise, parrots, kingfishers, cassowaries, pythons and other snakes, crocodiles, turtles, bats, rats, butterflies, and spiders
Plants: About 9,000 species of plants and trees, including oak, rosewood, kwila, ebony, walnut, and pine; Alpine grasses, orchids, ferns, and creepers

Land of Diversity

Papua New Guinea is one of the most isolated and fascinating areas of the world. Located in the South Pacific, it consists of the eastern half of New Guinea island and over 600 smaller islands. The total land mass is slightly bigger than California. An amazing variety of animals, plants, and insects live in the mountain highlands, dense rain forests, swamps, **savannas,** and coral reef-rimmed coasts.

This rugged landscape makes travel so difficult that people usually live in the same remote villages as their ancestors and may share few spiritual beliefs or traditions with other tribes. There are more than 750 different languages spoken, which makes the sharing of knowledge and cultures even more difficult. Today, most people speak Pidgin, a combination of different languages, including English. Government officials prefer that people use English. They feel this will help the country interact more easily with the rest of the world.

Tribal Society

Most people live very much as their ancestors did in simple tribal villages made up of families and **clans.** They live off the land, farming or fishing. Some communities trade goods. Houses are made of grass, wood, or bamboo, and may be grouped around a central area for community events. Men conduct community business and are responsible for heavy work like building, clearing land, and hunting. Women handle household chores, gardening, and care of the animals and children. In some areas, foreign businesses provide jobs in commercial farming, mining, and logging. There are a few cities, such as the capital, Port Moresby. It has a university, a national museum and art gallery, and an international airport. But even Port Moresby does not have roads leading to other urban areas. Canoes and boats are used to travel between villages located along the water. For most people, travel and communication are very difficult.

Houses with round ▶ thatch roofs stand in a row in a village in Papua New Guinea's highlands.

A Lack of Written History

No written history of Papua New Guinea exists before the arrival of the first Europeans in the 1500s. Human remains have been found in the interior of New Guinea dating back at least 10,000 years, but the region was probably settled around 50,000 years ago by people from Indonesia, Asia, and Australia. Little evidence remains from that time.

We know about many other ancient cultures from monuments, ruins, and artifacts found. But the people of Papua New Guinea built their houses and made tools and art from natural elements like wood, shells, tree bark, and leaves. This material decays very quickly in the hot, wet climate. The only information we know about the early history comes from the stories and traditional beliefs that have been passed down over many generations. Traditions are slowly being transformed by the introduction of the modern world, but the old beliefs and rituals remain an important part of Papua New Guinea culture.

The World Discovers Papua New Guinea

Europeans visited in the 16th century, but land claims did not begin until the Dutch took control of the western half of the island in the 19th century. Foreign explorers came to Papua New Guinea because of the area's rich natural resources and fascinating cultures. Along the Sepik River, explorers discovered tribes that made carvings in all kinds of objects. Everyday tools like jugs and canoe paddles were decorated, as well as special ceremonial masks and sculptures. These carvings honored the spirit world.

By 1900, Germany and Britain had claimed separate parts of eastern New Guinea. By 1918, after World War I, Australia had full control of the eastern half of the island. For over a century, Papua New Guinea was occupied by foreign governments. The country gained its independence in 1975, but even today, people feel more loyalty to their tribe than to the country's distant central government.

▲ The carving on the Parliament House in Port Moresby is in the traditional style of a *Haus Tambaran*.

House of Spirits

The most important place in many villages is the *Haus Tambaran,* or Spirit House, with its high, pointed **facade**. The carvings on the inside and outside of the house represent ancestors and great spirits. The Parliament House in Port Moresby is built in the traditional style of a *tambaran*.

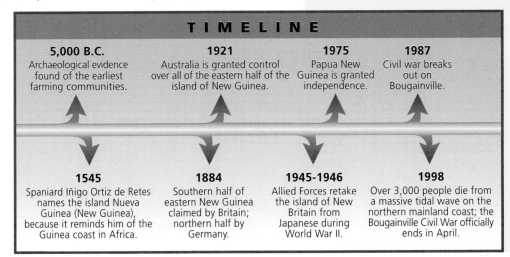

TIMELINE

5,000 B.C.
Archaeological evidence found of the earliest farming communities.

1921
Australia is granted control over all of the eastern half of the island of New Guinea.

1975
Papua New Guinea is granted independence.

1987
Civil war breaks out on Bougainville.

1545
Spaniard Iñigo Ortiz de Retes names the island Nueva Guinea (New Guinea), because it reminds him of the Guinea coast in Africa.

1884
Southern half of eastern New Guinea claimed by Britain; northern half by Germany.

1945-1946
Allied Forces retake the island of New Britain from Japanese during World War II.

1998
Over 3,000 people die from a massive tidal wave on the northern mainland coast; the Bougainville Civil War officially ends in April.

A Thousand Cultures

Spiritual beliefs, rules, and ways of life differ from village to village. All tribes, however, believe in the **supernatural,** although different tribes honor the spirit world in their own way. People from the Sepik River region, for example, decorate everyday objects to honor the spirits. Bowls, pots, canoes, and musical instruments have detailed and sometimes painted carvings of human figures, animals, and patterns. The people believe that the spirits will grow angry if they are forgotten. By paying tribute, the carved object and the user become filled with the spirit's power.

Objects like masks and boards are also created especially for ceremonies that honor important events like weddings, harvest festivals, and battles. The people believe that these carvings and ritual celebrations give them power and luck in the tasks ahead and help them lead successful and happy lives.

Crocodiles

The people of the Sepik River region believe that the crocodile created the Earth and its people. They decorate the bows of their canoes and other objects with carvings of crocodiles and make offerings to the river to pay respect.

Sing-Sings

Rituals to honor the spirit world are an important part of tribal culture. There are many kinds of ceremonies and festivals. One of the most popular and common events is called a *sing-sing.* These colorful festivals are used to celebrate many occasions, including marriages, births and deaths, harvest and planting seasons, sea journeys, trade, and warfare.

Tribal members put on elaborate decoration—colorful body and facial paint, brilliant headpieces sprouting bird feathers, and jewelry made from shells and beads. There is feasting, music, dancing, and storytelling. In the stories, participants play the role of natural elements, such as trees, rivers, and mountains, in addition to the characters. Sometimes fancy wooden masks or war shields are created to help tell a story. Stories may tell about the creation of the world, good and evil, the tribe's history, or great battles.

This woman and child ▶ are dressed to attend a *sing-sing* in their village.

The Art of War

Long ago, when tribes along the Sepik River went to war, warriors often carried special decorated shields. They hoped the ancestors, great warriors, and animal spirits carved on the shield would give them power. The faces on the shields sometimes featured large eyes and wide open mouths to frighten the enemy. Animal figures were often tribal totems of the animals believed to protect the tribe, like a snake, bird, or shark. Designs were often handed down through the family. Even geometric patterns had special meaning.

A Traditional Shield

▲ This shield is from the Upper Sepik River region.

Warriors used the wood from any hardwood tree or a panel from an old canoe to make their shields. Stone or iron axes cut and split the tree trunk. The piece was then shaped to fit over most of the body and thinned so it would not be too heavy. The wood was dried by hanging it over a small fire and tying ropes around it so it would bend slightly. The curve in the shield helped protect the warrior by making it fit closer to his body.

Small axes, animal teeth, nails, and bone **chisels** were used to carve human figures, faces, animal **motifs,** and geometric patterns in the shield. Burned shells, charcoal, and clay were used to make natural white, black, red, and brown colors to paint the shield. Finally, the shield was polished using grindstones, coral, or a wild boar **tusk.** When the shield was finished, a warrior felt confident going into battle.

Payback

A tribe is responsible for all of its members. If a tribe member injures a member of another tribe or their property, the entire tribe must make **compensation,** called *payback*. There are **negotiations** over payment, which traditionally is in the form of pigs. Failure to make payback is considered the worst possible offense and can lead to war.

A New Reason to Carve

Today, war is not very common, and many people have forgotten the meaning of the designs. The people of the Sepik River region now make shields and other carvings, like masks, pots, and sculptures, mostly to sell to tourists. These artisans combine traditional styles and their own imaginations to create their designs.

Drummers help tell a story as part of ▶ many celebrations and ceremonies.

Tools

- C-clamps
- old towel
- pencil
- wood chisels, 1/4-in. (1/2-cm) and wider
- wooden or rubber mallet
- rasp and file
- paintbrushes

Materials

- 3/4-in. (2-cm) cedar or pine boards; 1 small scrap and 1 board, 10 x 20 in. (25 x 50 cm) or larger
- paper
- acrylic paint (black, white, red oxide, yellow oxide)
- wax paper
- picture hanging bracket

Use simple woodcarving techniques to decorate a board in the bold style of artisans from Papua New Guinea.

Experiment with Woodcarving

In Papua New Guinea, woodcarvers decorate shields with carved designs. They also cut narrow grooves in the wood. After carving, the whole surface is painted with bold colors.

Experiment with the carving tools and techniques before you begin your own shield. Be sure to follow the safety guidelines at the right.

Carved Shapes

1. Clamp a scrap of wood tightly to a solid table. (You may want to protect the table with an old towel.)

2. Draw a simple shape such as a triangle on the wood with a pencil. Shade in the area inside the shape.

3. Grasp a wide chisel firmly by the handle, and hold it straight up and down. Put the cutting edge on the pencil line. Tap the chisel with the mallet. Cut about 1/8 inch (.3 cm) down into the wood. This vertical cut is called a *stop-cut. (See diagram.)*

4. Make stop-cuts along the outline of the triangle, all to the same depth. The stop-cuts will act as a barrier. They will keep the wood from splitting too far when you begin to carve away the area inside. *(See diagram.)*

> ### Woodcarving Safety
>
> - **Have an adult work with you.**
> - Learn the correct way to use a tool, and use it for its intended purpose only.
> - Always clamp the wood to a stable base before carving.
> - Use common sense! Never put your fingers in front of the chisel when you are carving. Cut away from yourself and others.

Carved Shapes

3. Make a stop-cut.

4. Make stop-cuts along the outline.

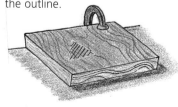

Clamp the wood and carve ▶ your shield in a safe way.

Tools

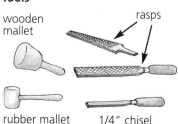

wooden mallet

rasps

rubber mallet

1/4" chisel

5. Now, use a *wedge-cut* to remove the wood inside the triangle. To make this cut, hold the chisel at a very low angle. Turn the beveled, or sloped, edge of the chisel up. Tap the chisel gently to chip up a thin sliver of wood. (If you hold the chisel at too steep an angle, it will wedge up too thick of a chunk.) *(See diagram.)*

6. Continue to carve out the wood inside the triangle. Take it down, one thin layer at a time, to the depth of your stop-cuts. It is easiest to carve in the same direction as the grain of the wood. This will also help to prevent splitting.

Carved Grooves

1. Try carving a narrow groove. Draw a small circle. Draw another circle around the first to create an even band 1/4-inch (1/2-cm) wide. Use a pencil to shade in the band. *(See diagram.)*

2. Use your narrowest chisel to make stop-cuts around both of the circles. Then carve out a groove between the stop-cuts. Hold the chisel at a low angle and tap it gently. Remember to carve in the same direction as the grain of the wood. *(See diagram.)*

Plan a Shield

Many shields in Papua New Guinea are decorated with abstract images of the human face. Other common patterns are shown at the right. The designs are large, bold, and brightly colored. They are meant to be seen in motion and from a distance. A display of many moving shields is dazzling!

1. Carving a shield takes effort and time. Use your experience with carving to help you plan. Make some drawings of your ideas. Draw patterns that you like and that you will be able to carve fairly easily.

2. Cut a large piece of paper that is the size of your shield. Draw the outside shape of the shield. It may be rectangular, or it may have rounded edges.

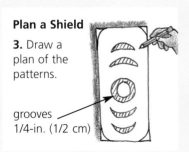

Plan a Shield

3. Draw a plan of the patterns.

grooves 1/4-in. (1/2 cm)

3. Draw an exact plan of the patterns on the shield. Make sure the shapes are separated enough to keep the wood from splitting. Draw grooves that are 1/4-inch (1/2-cm) or wider. Use the side of the pencil to shade in the areas that will be carved away. *(See diagram.)*

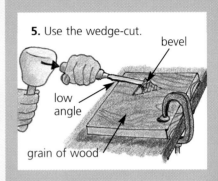

5. Use the wedge-cut.

bevel

low angle

grain of wood

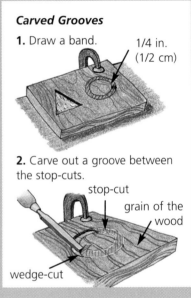

Carved Grooves

1. Draw a band.

1/4 in. (1/2 cm)

2. Carve out a groove between the stop-cuts.

stop-cut

grain of the wood

wedge-cut

Traditional Patterns in New Guinea

circles — zigzags

diamonds — half-moons

triangles — spirals

Carve a Shield

1. Cut the board.

file the edges

2. Trace over the lines.

Carving Hints

■ Use great care when you work with wood-carving tools. Always work with an adult present.

■ Use a narrow chisel for outlining curved areas and a wide chisel for outlining long straight areas.

■ If your chisels are dull, they will mash the wood rather than make a clean cut. Ask an adult to sharpen them.

■ If you accidentally carve out more wood than you intended, just change your design, or glue the chip back in place with wood glue.

Carve a Shield

1. Use dry wood to make your shield. Wet wood is very hard to carve. The board should have few knotholes and no splits at all. **Ask an adult to cut the board to the length and shape that you want.** File and round the edges with a rasp. File away any splinters. *(See diagram.)*

2. Lay your plan on the board. Check to make sure you won't be carving through a knothole. Trace over the lines, pushing hard enough to leave a dent in the wood. *(See diagram.)*

3. Redraw the cutting lines on the wood with a pencil. Shade the areas you want to carve away. Draw the design clearly to prevent carving away the wrong parts! *(See diagram.)*

3. Draw the design clearly.

4. Carve your shield. Read the carving hints on the left. Use great care when you work with wood-carving tools.

5. Use a narrow chisel to smooth the wood a little. You don't have to make the surfaces too smooth, since they will be painted.

6. Paint your shield. Refer to the Acrylic Paint Hints on page 15. The traditional colors used in Papua New Guinea are red, white, black, and yellow. If you want, you can paint some parts without carving them. Arrange the colors so that they contrast strongly. This will help the patterns to stand out.

7. Attach a picture bracket to the back of your shield. Then hang it on the wall.

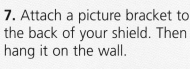

Three shields ▶ carved and painted by students.

This Maori carving shows facial tattooing, or *moko*. Legend tells of the Tattooed Rocks near Raglan.

Auckland, located on the North Island, is one of New Zealand's largest cities.

Mt. Ruapehu is an active volcano. It has erupted many times in the last ten years.

The kiwi is the only known bird with external nostrils in the tip of its bill. These nostrils help it to find food on the forest floor by smell. Kiwis are found at the Kiwi House in Napier.

PACIFIC OCEAN

Cape Reinga

TASMAN SEA

Great Barrier Island

Hauraki Gulf

Auckland

Waikato River

Bay of Plenty

East Cape

Raglan Harbour

Rotorua

NORTH ISLAND

Lake Taupo

Mount Ruapehu

Napier

Hawke Bay

NEW ZEALAND

Wellington

Cook Strait

Karamea Bight

Nelson

Cape Foulwind

SOUTH ISLAND

Christchurch

Mount Cook

Lake Pukaki

Canterbury Bight

Lake Hawea

Lake Wakatipu

Otago

Lake Te Anau

Dunedin

Foveaux Strait

Stewart Island

N
W E
S

0   150 miles
0   200 km

PACIFIC OCEAN

New Zealand

▲ New Zealand is made up of two volcanic islands with beautiful bays and waterways.

Land of the Long White Cloud

New Zealand, a green, mist-covered land in the southwest Pacific, is made up of two main volcanic islands: North Island and South Island. Smaller nearby island groups and a few subantarctic island groups farther south are also part of New Zealand.

Aotearoa is a Maori (Mah-OR-ee) name for New Zealand. It means the "land of the long white cloud." The Maori were the first inhabitants of New Zealand. Historians believe they came about A.D. 1000 or even earlier in large sailing canoes from islands in Eastern Polynesia in search of a new home. According to Maori legend, the hero Maui created New Zealand. He caught a huge fish that became the North Island. His canoe became the South Island. Stewart Island came from the anchor that held Maui's canoe as he hauled in the giant fish.

The First Settlers

Most of the early Maori settlers lived on the North Island. By 1300, settlements were established around most of the east coast. The first centuries of settlement in New Zealand were mostly peaceful. The Maori fished, hunted *moas*, and used stone and carved bone tools. They began to grow crops, mainly on the warmer North Island. The *kumara*, or sweet potato, is still grown today.

The Maori believed that land, canoes, houses, and other large possessions belonged to the tribe and not to individuals. They believed that land can sustain life, while human possessions cannot. Because of this, the early Maori had only a few personal possessions. As the Maori population increased and resources grew **scarce** in some areas, tensions increased. The Maori carefully protected and defended their land, and boundary disagreements caused quarrels between some tribes. As a result, settlements called *pa* were built on hills for easy defense. These settlements appeared around 1500.

Moas

Long ago, Maori hunted giant wingless birds called *moas*. *Moas* provided meat, large eggs, bones, and feathers. *Moas* were overhunted by the early Maori settlers and are now **extinct**.

Europeans Arrive

The first European to see New Zealand was a Dutch navigator named Abel Tasman. In 1642, he attempted to land on the South Island but was turned away by a **hostile** Maori tribe. He narrowly escaped but managed to document the first written account of New Zealand in his journal, which included writing and sketches.

It was over 100 years later, in 1769, that British explorer Captain James Cook sailed to New Zealand. Unlike Tasman, he managed to establish friendly relations with many Maori people. His glowing accounts helped spread the word that New Zealand was a good place to get land and to settle.

▲ The Maori suffered defeat and displacement when the Europeans arrived in the 19th century. Today the Maori people continue to practice and develop their communities and art forms.

The first Europeans to take Cook at his word were whalers and sealers. They arrived in the late 1700s, destroying New Zealand's whale and seal population. Within twenty years, the seal population was depleted. Whales were fished out by the end of the century.

Next came the traders. Huge amounts of New Zealand flax fiber could be traded for firearms, so many Maori tribes abandoned their hill *pa,* or settlements, to live for months in swampy land, gathering flax. These unhealthy living conditions led to outbreaks of diseases like tuberculosis. Many Maori also died from diseases brought by European traders.

By 1858, there were more European settlers than Maori. Being outnumbered drove the Maori to war. The Taranaki War of 1860 and the Waikato Campaign of 1863 resulted in defeat for the Maori. The last twenty years of the 1800s were a painful time for the Maori. The Europeans moved them off the tribal lands they had occupied for centuries. By the turn of the century, war and disease had decreased the Maori population to an all-time low of about 40,000.

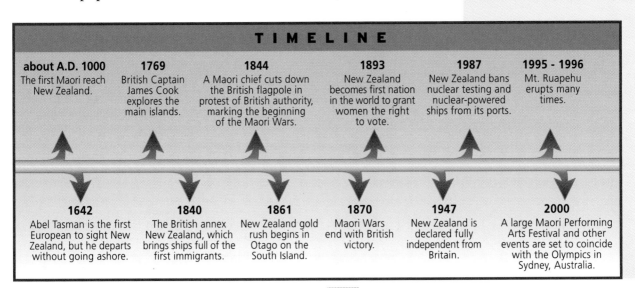

TIMELINE

about A.D. 1000
The first Maori reach New Zealand.

1769
British Captain James Cook explores the main islands.

1844
A Maori chief cuts down the British flagpole in protest of British authority, marking the beginning of the Maori Wars.

1893
New Zealand becomes first nation in the world to grant women the right to vote.

1987
New Zealand bans nuclear testing and nuclear-powered ships from its ports.

1995 - 1996
Mt. Ruapehu erupts many times.

1642
Abel Tasman is the first European to sight New Zealand, but he departs without going ashore.

1840
The British annex New Zealand, which brings ships full of the first immigrants.

1861
New Zealand gold rush begins in Otago on the South Island.

1870
Maori Wars end with British victory.

1947
New Zealand is declared fully independent from Britain.

2000
A large Maori Performing Arts Festival and other events are set to coincide with the Olympics in Sydney, Australia.

New Zealand Flax

When the Maori first arrived in New Zealand, they found the weather cooler than the **tropical** climate they had left in Polynesia. They needed garments that would protect them from the rain and chilly nights. In Polynesia, their clothing had come from plants and trees not found in New Zealand. The Maori settlers discovered New Zealand flax, a five- to six-foot tall, big-leafed plant. It grew abundantly in the North Island. The Maori used strips of the flax leaves to weave baskets and mats. This weaving was done by *plaiting*, or braiding, the fibers.

The plaited flax leaves were too rough and stiff to use for clothing, but by scraping the flax leaves across the sharp edge of a shell, the silky linen fibers, called *muka*, could be separated out and rolled into thread.

The flax had to be gathered properly at the right time and under the right conditions. Rain made the flax too wet. The wind made the flax fibers hard to remove, and frost made them too brittle. After the fibers were soaked, pounded, and bleached in the sun, they could be woven by hand into cloaks and other articles of clothing.

Since the Maori didn't have looms, they used an old Polynesian tying technique used for making fish traps called "finger weaving." The finest weaving was done on cloaks. The cloak was an important article of clothing to the Maori. Cloaks had borders with bands of fine weaving in three or four colors. These borders were called *taaniko*, a word that refers to the patterns as well as the weaving technique. Some objects and clothing were further decorated with feathers or dog hair.

New Zealand Flax

The early Maori settlers found many uses for New Zealand flax.

■ The sticky substance at the base of the leaves was used on burns.

■ The stalks served as torches or floats.

■ The rhizome, a part of the plant stem or root, was used as a medicine.

■ The leaves and leaf fibers were used to make cloaks, belts, nets, mats, and other objects.

The early Maori ▶ developed the method of "finger weaving."

Taaniko Patterns

Taaniko weaving is characterized by diagonal straight lines, perhaps because the triangle, zigzag, diamond, and pyramid were easier to weave than curved designs. It may also be because plaiting, a technique the Maori brought with them from Polynesia, was based on diagonal lines.

The early Maori were very skilled at making complex patterns. They had to keep the patterns in their head, since they didn't have graph paper to plan their designs. Later, graph paper made it easier to create new symbols, such as stars, the kiwi, ferns, and even words.

Facial Tattooing, an Ancient Maori Art Form

▲ The Maori were skilled at weaving complex geometric patterns such as the border on this skirt, which was made long ago.

▲ Historically, warriors had full facial tattoos. Today, performers create the same effect using face paint.

Facial tattooing, or *moko*, is one of the oldest and most famous Maori art forms. Intricate patterns and designs were chiseled or etched into the skin and then filled in with ink dye. Young Maori men started out with simple designs. As they grew older, more spiral designs were added as symbols of success in battle. Only very distinguished warriors had full facial tattoos. The practice of facial tattooing on men ended in the late 1800s.

Women's *moko* were much simpler. They were usually only on the lips or the tip of the nose, a practice that continued for women until the mid-1900s. Today, Maori performers use face paint to represent the tribal *moko* tradition in Maori history.

Tattooed Rocks

Whale Bay, near Raglan, is said to be the site of the Tattooed Rocks. According to legend, long ago a young Maori artist carved two large rocks on the beach. They are said to be visible only at low tide. Many people in the area have searched unsuccessfully for them for years.

Wooden flute

Air, Breath, Music, and Healing

The Maori believed air and breath to be the heart of life. These elements were celebrated and controlled through instruments and music. The flute, a wind instrument, came from the Maori goddess Hineraukatauri. Flute music and chants helped to soothe the pain of tattooing. Small discs on cords were spun over the joints of arthritis patients and over the chests of those with breathing problems.

Taaniko Dyes

The Maori dyed the flax thread before weaving it into geometric taaniko patterns. Their dyes came from prepared red and blue-white clays, pigments, swamp mud, plants, and trees. Most traditional taaniko borders used three colors—black, red/brown, and yellow—plus the natural undyed color of the flax fiber.

In the 19th century, designs were sometimes oversewn, using European needles and blue and red cotton thread. Over time, manufactured chemical dyes began to replace the vegetable dyes and soft colors that marked traditional taaniko borders.

Weaving Customs

In traditional Maori culture, older weavers watched young girls for signs of one who might be a weaver. An elder women in a family would teach a young girl who was believed to be a weaver.

It is expected that a weaver will give away her first completed weaving, often to the senior member of the family. At other times the weaving may instead be buried, giving it back to mother earth. The weaver knows to whom a weaving will go before she begins. This helps her to concentrate on the weaving, the person, and the process. When the weaving is completed, thanks is given.

Custom discourages a weaver from teaching anyone older than herself. If she does, it is considered sharing, rather than teaching. Another custom respects the weaver's need for privacy as she completes the first row of weaving. This row takes great concentration, because it is in the first row that the pattern for the entire weaving is created.

▲ Today, people work on taaniko as they might a piece of knitting—on trains, during meetings, or while waiting for the bus.

◄ Clothing with taaniko weaving is worn with great pride.

Artistic Roles

Traditionally, Maori women usually worked with soft materials. They wove clothes and made mats and baskets. The men worked with hard materials, such as wood, stone, and bone. They were expert carvers.

The Maori Today

The Maori people believe that the past, the "ever-present now," lives in the present and the future. It is through art forms such as weaving and carving that many Maori beliefs are passed down to future generations.

Taonga—A Living Force

Maori artists are challenged to take material objects as large as a carved meeting house or as small as a tiny bone fishing lure to the level of *taonga*, which means "highly treasured or sacred object." To the Maori, the world is like a big family tree where everything is connected. The Maori treat their art objects as people who have a history and a life force. They, along with the artists who create them, occupy a special place in tribal history. *Taonga* also includes the myths, traditions, memories, and stories that represent Maori culture.

▲ Fishing is an important source of food. Carved fishhooks made of greenstone are prized possessions.

The Importance of Words

The Maori had no written language. They preserved and passed down their knowledge through oral tradition. The Maori liked to play with words. They told riddles, proverbs, and puzzles, making up new ones daily to entertain each other. They also used storytelling, songs, and chants to convey their tribe's history and values to its youngest members.

The Meeting House

The carved Maori meeting house is *taonga*. The meeting house represents an ancestor's body who holds a special place in tribal history. The ridgepole represents the spine, the middle rafters the ribs, and the front beams the arms. The meeting house contains all of a tribe's history. It symbolizes community and offers support and shelter to those who enter.

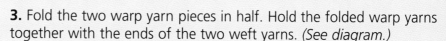

Project: *Taaniko* Woven Band

Tools

- scissors
- colored pencils
- large tapestry needle

Materials

- colorful yarns
- smooth cotton cord or twine
- small piece of beeswax
- rubber bands
- masking tape
- graph paper

Make a bracelet using simplified Maori weaving techniques. You can carry this project anywhere. No loom is needed!

Prepare to Weave

1. First, choose the two colors of *weft* yarns that will make the pattern. Read the hints at the right. Cut a six-foot (2 m) piece of each color you choose.

2. Next, choose the *warp* yarn, the vertical pieces to build your pattern on. It's easier to weave if the warp is a bit stiffer than the weft yarns. Smooth cotton cord or twine works well. You can stiffen softer yarn by rubbing it on beeswax. Cut two pieces of warp yarn, each two feet (60 cm) long.

3. Fold the two warp yarn pieces in half. Hold the folded warp yarns together with the ends of the two weft yarns. *(See diagram.)*

4. Tie a big overhand knot. Leave a small loop above the knot, and six strands of yarn below. *(See diagram.)*

5. Wrap the long, loose ends of the weft yarns into two small bundles. Fasten them with rubber bands.

6. Tape the loop to the edge of a table. Pull the pair of weft yarns over to the left. You are ready to weave! *(See diagram.)*

Color Hints

- The pattern will stand out best if the colors strongly contrast.

- Traditional Maori colors are red, black, white, and yellow.

Prepare to Weave

3. Hold the ends together.

4. Tie a big overhand knot.

loop

overhand knot

6. You are ready to weave.

2 weft yarn bundles

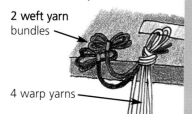

4 warp yarns

One-Color Weaving

2. Insert the first warp yarn.

first warp yarn

weft yarns

One-Color Weaving

Taaniko is a kind of finger weaving sometimes called twining. Your fingers will need to learn a coordinated set of movements. Start with a few rows of one-color weaving to learn how to hold and twist the yarns. It may seem hard at first, but just keep practicing.

1. In your right hand, hold the pair of weft yarns. Keep the two yarns separated with your thumb and first finger. Pull them horizontally over the four warp yarns.

2. Insert the first (left-most) warp yarn between the weft yarns. Clamp the first warp in your left hand, and pull it tight. *(See diagram.)*

3. Now you are ready to twist! With your right hand, turn the weft yarns clockwise (away from your body). Make the same movement you use to open a door knob. Make one complete twist, so that the same color of weft is facing you again. *(See diagram.)*

4. Hook the second warp yarn with one of your free fingers. Insert it between the weft yarns, as before. Grab it with your left hand and hold it stretched tight. *(See diagram.)*

5. Each place where the weft crosses the warp is called a *weft stitch.* Now you have two weft stitches, both the same color. Push them up firmly. You will probably see a little bit of the bottom weft yarn between the stitches. Tug firmly on the bottom weft so that it disappears to the back. *(See diagram.)*

6. Repeat Steps 3 through 5 until you have four weft stitches. The four warp yarns are now all in your left hand. Push all the stitches up to the top. Twist the weft once more to close the edge. You have finished one row of weaving. *(See diagram.)*

7. Now you will weave back in the other direction. Insert the fourth warp yarn back between the weft yarns. Switch hands, holding the weft yarns in your left hand and the fourth warp yarn in your right hand. *(See diagram.)*

8. Twist the weft yarns clockwise as before, but with your left hand instead of your right (this time, *toward* your body). It will still be the same movement you make to open a door knob. *(See diagram.)*

9. Continue with one-color weaving until you feel ready to begin the pattern.

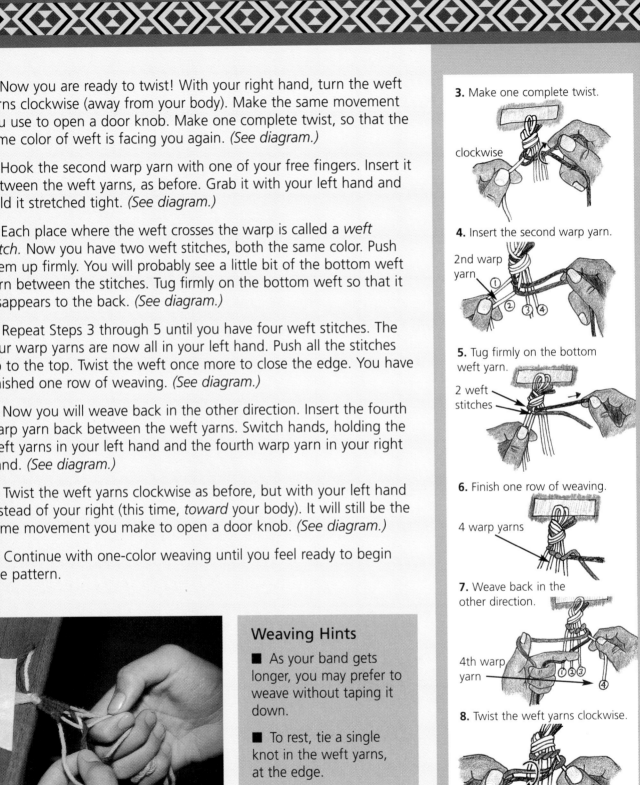

3. Make one complete twist.

clockwise

4. Insert the second warp yarn.

2nd warp yarn

5. Tug firmly on the bottom weft yarn.

2 weft stitches

6. Finish one row of weaving.

4 warp yarns

7. Weave back in the other direction.

4th warp yarn

8. Twist the weft yarns clockwise.

Weaving Hints

■ As your band gets longer, you may prefer to weave without taping it down.

■ To rest, tie a single knot in the weft yarns, at the edge.

◄ Starting a band with one-color weaving.

Pattern Weaving

1. Plan the pattern, and make a chart. Study the examples illustrated here for ideas. Outline a section of graph paper four squares wide. Each square represents one weft stitch. *(See diagram.)*

2. Color the squares with two colors of pencils to chart the pattern. Chart a short section that will repeat to the end of your band.

3. Begin to weave the pattern from either edge. Weave as before, but change colors by twisting the weft yarns only one-half twist. This will leave the back weft at the front. The key to taaniko weaving is to use **one full twist to keep the same color and one-half twist to change colors.** *(See diagram.)*

4. Continue to weave. Follow the pattern chart back and forth, just like you weave.

5. Stop when your band is long enough to fit around your wrist comfortably. Tie the weft yarns together at the edge. Cut the extra weft off, leaving a long tail. Use a large tapestry or carpet needle to weave the weft ends into the back of the band. *(See diagram.)*

6. Tie the ends of the four warp yarns in a large overhand knot. Trim off the ends. Attach your band to your wrist by tucking the knot into the loop. *(See diagram.)*

Pattern Weaving

1. Make a pattern chart.

chevron   diagonal stripes

triangles   stripes

3. To change colors, twist one half twist.

5. Weave the weft ends into the back.

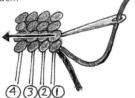

6. Tie the warp yarns into a large knot.

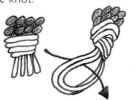

Taaniko bands ▶ woven by students.

Other Ideas

■ Use cotton embroidery floss weft yarns for a delicate look.

■ Use six or eight warp yarns for a wider band for a headband or belt.

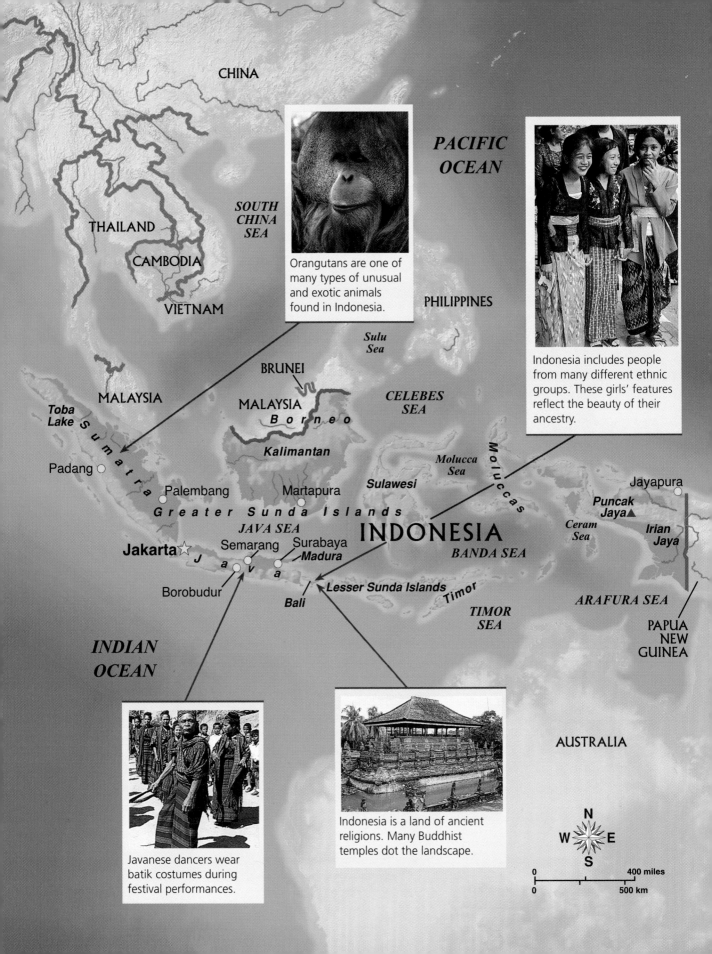

CHINA

PACIFIC
OCEAN

SOUTH
CHINA
SEA

THAILAND

CAMBODIA

VIETNAM

Orangutans are one of
many types of unusual
and exotic animals
found in Indonesia.

PHILIPPINES

Indonesia includes people
from many different ethnic
groups. These girls' features
reflect the beauty of their
ancestry.

Sulu
Sea

BRUNEI

MALAYSIA

Toba
Lake

Padang

MALAYSIA
Borneo

CELEBES
SEA

S u m a t r a

Kalimantan

*Molucca
Sea*

Moluccas

Jayapura

Palembang

Martapura

Sulawesi

Puncak
Jaya▲

Greater   Sunda   Islands

INDONESIA

*Ceram
Sea*

*Irian
Jaya*

JAVA SEA

Semarang

Surabaya

BANDA SEA

Jakarta☆   *J*

a

Madura

v

a

Borobudur

Lesser Sunda Islands

Timor

ARAFURA SEA

Bali

TIMOR
SEA

PAPUA
NEW
GUINEA

INDIAN
OCEAN

AUSTRALIA

Javanese dancers wear
batik costumes during
festival performances.

Indonesia is a land of ancient
religions. Many Buddhist
temples dot the landscape.

N
W ☀ E
S

0   400 miles
0   500 km

Indonesia

Indonesia Facts

Name: Indonesia, an island republic in Southeast Asia, made up of more than 13,500 islands
Capital: Jakarta
Borders: World's largest island complex, surrounded by the Indian Ocean, the Pacific Ocean, and many seas; nearest countries: Philippines, Malaysia, Australia, Papua New Guinea; (The western half of New Guinea is Indonesia's easternmost province, Irian Jaya)
Population: Over 212 million (world's fourth largest population)
Language: Official language: Bahasa Indonesian; 668 languages and dialects spoken
Size: 782,705 sq. mi. (2,027,206 sq km)
High/Low Points: Puncak Jaya, 16,524 ft. (5,030 m); sea level along the coasts
Climate: Continually hot, wet weather; sea level temperatures are about 78-82° F (25-28° C); a dry season only in the southern islands; year-round snow on the highest peaks
Wildlife: Orangutans, echidnas, tigers, flying foxes, tree kangaroos, sun bears, barking deer, and mouse deer; reptiles include komodo dragons, crocodiles, king cobras, pythons, and boa constrictors; many birds, including pea fowls, 45 species of kingfishers, kooka-burras, cassowaries, 72 species of parrots
Plants: Hundreds of species of plants and trees; flowers include orchids, Javanese edelweiss, and Rafflesia arnoldii (the world's largest flower, with a blossom three feet wide)

Land of Islands

Imagine sailing past thousands of islands, large and small, without ever leaving your country! The entire Indonesian nation is an **archipelago** of more than 13,500 islands covering 3,000 miles. Volcanic action helped to shape this chain of islands.

▲ Volcanoes have affected Indonesia in many ways throughout its history.

The Impact of Volcanoes

Indonesia holds the world record for the country with the most volcanoes, with about 70 active ones. Some eruptions have destroyed coastal villages, yet the volcanoes also help Indonesians. The volcanic ash replaces nutrients washed from the soil by heavy rainfall. As the soil becomes fertile, farmers move to those areas to grow crops. Farming is important. The land must supply a lot of food to feed Indonesia's growing population, most of whom live on the islands of Java, Madura, and Bali. Java, roughly as big as New York State, has 107 million people, with a very dense rural population.

Boatloads Full of Batik

The deep seas and high mountains formed by volcanic action helped to isolate Indonesia's many cultural groups from one another, so it is easy to see how different groups mastered different skills and crafts. The Sumatrans made masks for ritual dances. The tribal warriors of Irian Jaya and Borneo made swords and carved shields. The central islanders made sacred swords called *kris*. And the people on Java made shadow puppets and decorative **textiles** called *batik*.

The word batik (buh TEEK) means to arrange by dots or to write with wax. It is a process of making patterns on cloth. The completed fabric looks a little like what Americans call "tie-dye," but the process is far from new. People have made batik for many centuries.

The people of Java were skilled at sailing as well as creating batik. They loaded up their boats with the beautiful cloth and other goods and set sail to trade with people throughout Southeast Asia. Javanese batik soon became famous worldwide.

Stepping Stones of Southeastern Asia

A giant walking from Asia to Australia could use the Indonesian islands as stepping stones. Through the centuries, these islands have been stepping stones for people traveling throughout Southeast Asia.

▲ Religious celebrations help Indonesians keep ancient beliefs and traditions alive.

Travelers would stop off at various islands. In the process, they exchanged art, goods, and religion with the Indonesian people.

Indonesia's name reflects its close ties with both India and Asia. Beginning 4,500 years ago, settlers from east Asia or the Pacific islands began to stream onto the coasts of Indonesia. Much later, Indians arrived and introduced the Hindu and Buddhist religions. More Indian and Arab travelers often visited the islands during the 13th century. They expanded trade and brought in the now-official religion of Islam. Finally, in the 16th century, Portuguese, British, and Dutch people came to claim Indonesia as their home.

Trading Traditions

In the 17th century, traders from Malabar, India, exported great quantities of painted textiles to Java. The Javanese people decided it would be better to make and sell their own batik. They perfected their skills until batik became their national craft. To this day, the festivals of Java display the elegant taste and sense of color of the people who make and wear batik.

Religion and Batik

Animals such as the powerful lion and elephant play important roles in legends and in artwork. Due to Islamic beliefs, artists were not permitted to create living forms. But even then, Javanese batik artisans, or craftspeople, found solutions. They created elephants that looked like piles of rocks.

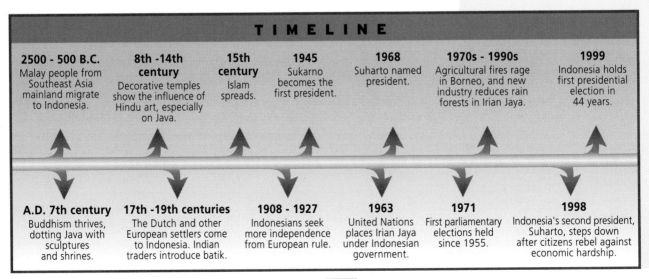

TIMELINE

2500 - 500 B.C.
Malay people from Southeast Asia mainland migrate to Indonesia.

8th -14th century
Decorative temples show the influence of Hindu art, especially on Java.

15th century
Islam spreads.

1945
Sukarno becomes the first president.

1968
Suharto named president.

1970s - 1990s
Agricultural fires rage in Borneo, and new industry reduces rain forests in Irian Jaya.

1999
Indonesia holds first presidential election in 44 years.

A.D. 7th century
Buddhism thrives, dotting Java with sculptures and shrines.

17th -19th centuries
The Dutch and other European settlers come to Indonesia. Indian traders introduce batik.

1908 - 1927
Indonesians seek more independence from European rule.

1963
United Nations places Irian Jaya under Indonesian government.

1971
First parliamentary elections held since 1955.

1998
Indonesia's second president, Suharto, steps down after citizens rebel against economic hardship.

Cities and Rain Forests

The geography of Indonesia varies along with the culture. Sixty percent of the people live on Java, where not an inch of land goes to waste. Gleaming green rice paddies cover the fields and hills between cities. In large cities like Jakarta, merchants sell paintings, batik, and souvenirs just a short distance from the rice paddies.

The islands of Borneo and Sumatra are less populated than Java. The most remote tribes can be found in the isolated rain forests of Irian Jaya, which borders Papua New Guinea. The cloud-capped mountains hid the Irian Jaya settlements from view until the 1950s when missionaries explored the land.

The plant resources of the Irian Jaya rain forest now help support the Indonesian economy. Indonesia exports lumber, medicinal plants, and even palm oil. The hand lotion at the supermarket may contain palm oil collected from trees in Indonesian forests.

Secret Recipes From Plants

Long ago, the people also learned the secrets of using plants to make batik. First, they washed the fabric in coconut oil until it turned cream-colored. Then they applied beeswax collected from hives in the forest. They used thin, hollow pieces of bamboo to drip the wax onto the cloth. (Later on, a *canting*, a special tool used for drawing with wax, was used. It made it easier to drip the wax and make detailed patterns.) Finally, they dipped the cloth in dyes made from plants, roots, and leaves.

Local customs, as well as the availability of plants, affected the choice of dyes. The earliest Javanese dye, blue indigo, came from the leaves of various plants. The indigo dye worked well because it resisted blending with the lighter colored fabric. In parts of central Java, people preferred brown dyes made from tree bark. Elsewhere, green and yellow dyes became popular. Dye recipes changed slowly over centuries. Batik makers guarded their dye recipes from rival countries.

Working Together

Indonesian people work together. Families share irrigation to grow rice. Between planting seasons, they prepare for ceremonies and create batik. In some areas, communities team up to make batik. One village may be best at waxing, while the neighboring village is best at dyeing.

Traditional Batik Tools

cloth a natural-fiber cloth, such as cotton

frame a wood frame to help hold the fabric in place

canting *(tjanting)* a copper cup fitted with spouts and set on a handle; used to drip the wax and make the designs

wax beeswax, sometimes with paraffin added

dye boiled dyes from these plants: red—bark and roots of the morinda tree or wood shavings from the sepang (sappan) tree; orange-red—bruguiera tree; yellow—safflower petals, turmeric root, or shavings from the jackfruit tree; blue—indigo plant; brown—tree barks mixed with indigo

cap a stamping tool used to make a border design

canting

A Belief in Balance

Indonesians care deeply about living in harmony with nature and with the community. The clothing worn, the dances danced, and the concerts and dramas performed all help to preserve this balance. Early batik artisans favored the soft colors, hoping the garment would keep the wearer in gentle harmony with his or her environment.

Designs and Patterns

Countries that traded with Indonesia introduced the early designs. The Chinese brought motifs, or themes that recur, such as clouds and earth symbols. Batik from India featured scenes from the life of the Hindu god Vishnu. The frequent use of birds and wings may have come from stories about Vishnu's eagle. Another symbol, the snake, possessed magical powers in both Hindu and Indonesian myths.

Gradually, Java developed its own guidelines for batik patterns. Everyday clothing had vertical or horizontal lines. Only high-ranking **aristocrats** or royalty could wear diagonal lines. Between the rows of lines, artisans added circles, squares, and stars. They placed plant or animal motifs inside these shapes. The designs that fill these circles or squares are called *isen*.

▲ Harmony with nature is an important theme. It is often seen in Indonesian art such as this sea life batik.

How Batik Has Changed

The Javanese people still care deeply about preserving their traditions. However, they now use tools to make the production of batik easier. They mix their dyes with chemicals instead of plants. They use machines to manufacture wider bolts of fabric, so they can make batik furniture and modern clothing. Even the patterns have changed somewhat as manufacturers accept newer and more original designs. One modern artisan draws inspiration from the artist Picasso! In spite of these changes, one tradition has stayed the same. People come from all over the world to buy the beautiful cloth of Java.

Tips for Batik Makers

Indonesians make batik clothing by dripping hot wax in dots, lines, and shapes onto cotton cloth. They dip the cloth in boiled dye. The wax resists the dye, or prevents it from coloring the area it covers, so artists refer to this method as resist dyeing. After they remove the wax, the color of the unbleached cloth shows where the wax once was. The wax must completely soak through the cloth or veins of dye will seep into the design.

Project: Batik Wall Hanging

Tools

- electric hot plate
- scissors
- hammer and chisel
- 2 small pots, 1 lid
- cooking thermometer
- pot holders
- colored chalk
- old towels
- old paintbrushes
- canting (optional), available at art stores
- smock or apron
- wide plastic tub
- dust mask
- measuring spoons, cups
- dye-mixing container
- rubber gloves
- large kettle
- large metal spoon
- empty soup can
- colored pencils
- sewing machine

Materials

- newspaper
- white 100% cotton muslin or sheeting, prewashed
- waxed paper
- beeswax and paraffin, 1 pound, (454 g) each
- paper towels
- cold-water dyes or batik dyes, available at art stores or by mail order (see Resources)
- non-iodized salt, soda ash
- laundry soap
- pencil and white paper
- dressmaker's transfer paper
- bamboo stick

Use the batik process to create a beautiful and colorful hanging for your wall.

Prepare the Materials

1. Cover a table with several layers of newspapers to catch drips of wax. Plug in the hot plate. Set it on the table so that you can reach it easily.

2. Cut and iron a piece of white fabric. Spread it flat on the newspapers. Put waxed paper under the fabric to keep it from sticking.

3. Break the beeswax and paraffin into small chunks with a hammer and chisel. Put a few chunks of each into a small pot.

4. Attach the cooking thermometer to the edge of the wax pot. The end of the thermometer should reach the wax, but not touch the bottom of the pot.

5. Fill another slightly larger pot with a little water. Set the wax pot inside the water pot, creating a double boiler.

6. Simmer the water until the wax melts. The water allows the wax to melt slowly and evenly. Follow the wax safety guidelines above.
Ask an adult to help you watch the temperature of the wax.

Wax Safety

- **You must have an adult work with you.**
- Tie your hair back and roll up your sleeves.
- Move slowly and carefully when working near hot wax.
- **Keep the temperature of the wax below 300°F (150°C).** Above this temperature, the wax will begin to smoke and could ignite into flames.
- Never leave the wax unattended when it is heating.
- If the wax should catch on fire, use a pan lid to smother the flames. **Never** pour water on it. Have a fire extinguisher nearby, just in case.

Batik Tools

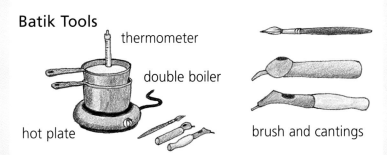

thermometer

double boiler

hot plate

brush and cantings

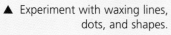

▲ Experiment with waxing lines, dots, and shapes.

Experiment with Batik

Wax and dye a small test design before you make your wall hanging. Have fun dabbling with the unfamiliar tools and materials. Make a design with a variety of shapes, dots, and lines. Try using Javanese *isen* designs in the background. *(See diagram.)*

1. Draw a design on the fabric with colored chalk. Outline the areas where you will apply the wax. These areas will stay white when you dye the fabric. *(See diagram.)*

2. The wax soaks into the fabric best at a temperature between 260° and 300° F (130-150° C). It won't get hot enough when it's in the water pot. Use a pot holder to remove the double boiler from the burner. Set it on a thick towel. **Have an adult help you wipe the bottom of the wax pot with a paper towel.** Then put the pot directly on the burner.

3. Have an adult help you. Watch the thermometer carefully. The wax will heat quickly. When it reaches the correct temperature, turn off the heat. If the temperature continues to rise, remove the pot from the burner. Continue to adjust the wax temperature as you work.

4. Dip a brush in the wax. If the brush is stiff with dry wax, wait for it to soften. Hold a paper towel under the brush to prevent drips. Quickly brush the wax on the fabric within the lines you drew. The hot wax will spread as it soaks into the fabric. It takes practice to control where it goes.

5. Try using a canting. Hold it in the hot wax for a moment so that the metal bowl is heated. Scoop just a little wax into the bowl. Tip the bowl back so the wax can't drip out of the spout.

6. Slide the spout of the canting smoothly along the surface of the fabric. Draw quickly to make thin lines, and slowly to make thicker lines. Try making some dots, also. If the wax flows out of the canting too quickly, use slightly cooler wax. *(See diagram.)*

7. When you are finished waxing, turn the fabric over. Peel off the wax paper. Check for places that the wax didn't penetrate. Wax over these places on the back, or the dye will run underneath them.

8. Take the brushes and canting out of the wax pot. Lay them flat on wax paper to dry.

Experiment with Batik

Background *isen* designs.

1. Draw a design.

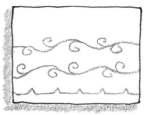

6. Draw lines with a canting.

Helpful Hints

■ If the wax is hot enough, it will seep into the fabric and look clear. If the wax is too cool, it will look milky and will peel off easily.

■ If you accidentally drip wax where you did not want it, you will need to be creative! Perhaps you can change the drip into a star or a pattern of dots.

▲ Lift and turn the fabric so that it dyes evenly.

Remove the Wax

2. Carefully skim the wax off the top.

Dye the Fabric

The most commonly used colors in Indonesia are brown, indigo blue, and white. Use dyes labeled for "cold water" or "batik." They must work in warm water, since the wax will melt in boiling water.

1. Follow the instructions on the dye package. Fill a wide dye tub with water no warmer than 110° F (43° C). Use a big enough tub and enough water to allow the fabric to float freely. You will need about one gallon (4 liters) for each square yard (sq m) of fabric.

2. Add salt to the water. Stir it until it disappears. Salt helps to drive the dye into the fabric. The amount of salt will vary with different dyes. Some dyes also need soda ash to make them work.

3. Ask an adult to measure the dye powder for you. Generally, you will need one teaspoon (3 g) of dye powder per gallon (4 liters) of water. Mix the dye with a little hot water in a plastic container until it is liquid. Add it to the dye tub.

4. Soak the waxed fabric in clear water for five minutes. Wet fabric will soak up the dye more evenly than dry fabric. If you want, crumple some areas of wax a little. Dye will seep into the tiny cracks in the wax, creating the typical veined look of batik.

5. Add the fabric to the tub. Wearing rubber gloves, reach into the dye. Gently smooth the fabric and mix the dye. Lift and turn the fabric every 10 to 15 minutes. When done, rinse the fabric well.

Remove the Wax

1. Boiling is the best way to remove wax. Fill a large pot with water and add the dyed fabric. Bring the water to a rapid boil. **Boiling water can be dangerous. Ask an adult to work with you.**

2. Boil for ten minutes. The wax will begin to melt and float to the surface. Carefully skim the wax off the top of the water with a large metal spoon. Put it in an empty soup can. *(See diagram.)*

3. When most of the wax has been removed, add a sprinkle of laundry soap to the pot. This will help remove most of the remaining wax. Skim off the soap and wax together.

4. Lift the hot fabric with the spoon. Put it in a tub of cold water to shock any remaining wax. Remove it by rubbing. Wash the fabric and dry. Don't pour the waxy water down the sink drain! Let it cool, skim the wax out, and then pour it outside.

Plan a Wall Hanging

Now that you have experimented with the batik process, you can get creative with color. Overdyeing layers of color is what makes batik so exciting! Plan a design that uses white plus two colors.

1. Make a pattern. Cut a piece of paper to the size of your wall hanging. Draw your design with pencil. Begin with simple shapes, and then add delicate *isen* patterns to fill the background. In Java, designs come from nature. Flowers, vines, fruits, birds, butterflies, and fish are common. *(See diagram.)*

2. To plan a multicolored batik, you must understand how colors mix. The second dye added to the first dye will result in a new color. Red over blue will make purple, and so on. Study the chart below. Also read the hints at the right.

2nd DYE	1st DYE					
	Red	**Orange**	**Yellow**	**Green**	**Light Blue**	**Light Purple**
Dark Red	Dark Red	Red Orange	Orange	Brown	Purple	Red Violet
Dark Orange	Red Orange	Dark Orange	Yellow Orange	Olive Green	Gray	Brown
Green	Dark Brown	Olive Green	Yellow Green	Dark Green	Blue Green	Dull Gray
Blue	Purple	Dull Gray	Dark Green	Blue Green	Dark Blue	Blue Violet
Purple	Red Violet	Dull Purple	Dark Brown	Dull Purple	Plum	Dark Purple
Black	Maroon	Dark Brown	Brown	Forest Green	Navy	Dark Purple

3. Choose your colors. Mark the pattern with colored pencils to show exactly where each color will go. *(See diagram.)*

4. It is hard to guess the results of dye combinations without testing them first. Make a dye test. Wax one area of a scrap of white fabric. Mix a little of your first color. Dye the test, then let it dry. Wax over a bit of the first color. Dye the second color. Boil off the wax and study the results. *(See diagram.)*

Make a Wall Hanging

1. Cut the fabric.

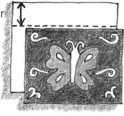

2. Copy the white areas to the fabric.

3. Wax the white areas.

6. Wax the medium color areas.

10. Sew a hem and hang.

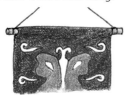

Other Ideas

- Try a three-color batik!
- Make a batik pillow.

Make a Wall Hanging

Making a batik takes patience. Each differently colored part of the design must be waxed and then dyed. In Java, complex designs take as many as 20 waxing and dyeing steps!

1. Cut the fabric to the size of your pattern. Add an extra four inches (10 cm) at the top to wrap around a bamboo stick. Iron the fabric. *(See diagram.)*

2. Copy the white areas of your design to the fabric with dressmaker's transfer paper. Sandwich the transfer paper between the pattern and the fabric, as shown in the illustration. Trace around only the white areas. *(See diagram.)*

3. Wax the white areas. *(See diagram.)*

4. Dye the first color (the medium color). Let the fabric dry thoroughly on an old towel or newspapers.

5. Now copy the parts of your design that will remain the medium color.

6. Wax the medium color areas to save them. Also look over the first waxed areas. Touch up any thin spots or places where the wax is loose. *(See diagram.)*

7. Wet the fabric and crumple the wax if you wish. Cracks will look better in large simple areas than in areas with fine lines.

8. Dye the second, darker color.

9. Remove the wax. Wash and dry the fabric.

10. Fold the top edge under and sew a wide hem. Insert the bamboo to hang your batik on the wall. Add a string or ribbon if desired. *(See diagram.)*

Batik wall hangings ▶ made by students.

Glossary

archipelago a group of many islands, or a sea containing such a group

aristocrats the wealthy, privileged class of society

artisans people who are skilled in an art, a craft, or a trade

chisel a metal tool with a cutting edge at the end of the blade

clan people who trace their descent from the same ancestor

cloak cape or robe

compensation making up for something, payment

extinct no longer existing

facade the face, or front, of a building

hostile vicious, warlike

immunity the ability to resist a disease

monsoon seasonal weather characterized by very heavy rainfall

motif a repeated design or theme in a work of art

negotiation discussion or conference in order to reach an agreement

ochre an earthy red or yellow, usually impure, iron ore used as a substance that colors

outback the dry, remote rural part, or interior, of Australia

plateau a level land surface raised sharply above land next to it on at least one side

prosperous successful, fortunate, well-off

savannas flat, mostly treeless grasslands

scarce not plentiful; in short supply

settlements new communities, sometimes formed by a government body to house a group of people removed from their homeland

supernatural appearing to be beyond what is normal or able to be explained by the laws of nature

textile hand-woven or machine-knitted cloth

tropical uniformly warm and mild weather, often having high temperatures and high humidity

tusk a long, pointed tooth that extends outside the mouth

Abbreviation Key

sq.	square
mi.	miles
km	kilometers
ft.	feet
m	meters
in.	inches
cm	centimeters
F	Fahrenheit
C	Centigrade
g	grams
ml	milliliters

Resources

Australia

Crumlin, Rosemary, and Anthony Knights, eds. *Aboriginal Art and Spirituality.* San Francisco: Harper, 1991

Darian-Smith, Kate. *Australia and Oceania.* Austin, TX: Raintree Steck-Vaughn, 1997

Lowe, David, and Andrea Shimmen. *Australia,* "Modern Industrial World" series. Austin TX: Raintree Steck-Vaughn, 1996

Nile, Richard. *Australian Aborigines,* "Threatened Cultures" series. Austin, TX: Raintree Steck-Vaughn, 1993

Nile, Richard, and Christian Clerk. *Cultural Atlas of Australia, New Zealand, and the Southwest Pacific.* New York: Facts on File, 1996

Sutton, Peter. *Dreamings: The Art of Aboriginal Australia.* New York: George Braziller, 1997

New Zealand

Kaula, Edna M. *The Land and People of New Zealand,* rev. ed., "Portraits of the Nations" series. New York: HarperCollins, 1964

Keyworth, Valerie. *New Zealand: Land of the Long White Cloud,* 2nd ed., "Discovering Our Heritage" series. Parsippany, NJ: Dillon, 1998

Macdonald, Robert. *Maori*, "Threatened Cultures" series. Austin, TX: Raintree Steck-Vaughn, 1994
Smith, Joyce Ronald. *Taaniko: Maori Hand-Weaving*. New York: Charles Scribner's Sons, 1975

Papua New Guinea
Bridgewater, Alan, and Gill Bridgewater. *A Treasury of Woodcarving Designs*. New York: Van Nostrand Reinhold, 1981
Lipscomb, Adrian, et al. *Papua/New Guinea*, 6th ed. Oakland, CA: Lonely Planet, 1998
MacDonald, Robert. *Islands of the Pacific Rim and Their People*. Austin, TX: Raintree Steck-Vaughn, 1994
Wardell, Allen, et al. *People of the River, People of the Tree: Change and Continuity in Sepik and Asmat Art*. Minneapolis: Minnesota Museum of Art, 1989

Indonesia
Arnott, Susi. *Indonesia*, "World Focus" series. Portsmouth, NH: Heinemann, 1997
Elliott, Inger McCabe. *Batik: Fabled Cloth of Java*. New York: Clarkson N. Potter, 1984
Jacobs, Judy. *Indonesia: A Nation of Islands*, "Discovering Our Heritage" series. Parsippany, NJ: Dillon, 1990
Lyle, Garry. *Indonesia*, "Major World Nations" series. Broomall, PA: Chelsea House, 1998
Smith, Datus C., Jr. *The Land and People of Indonesia*, rev. ed., "Portrait of the Nations" series. New York:HarperCollins, 1983

Index

Acknowledgments

Special thanks to these students for their time and energy in making the project samples: Anandi, Anna, Carrie B., Carrie S., Eleanor, Eva, Jessica, Justin, Laurel, and Louis; and to Jacob and Tim for their help. Thanks also to Jefferson Middle School, Eugene, Oregon; Teresa Langness; Diane Cissel, Terragraphics; Stephen Reynolds; Libris Solar; City Copy; Percy Franklin; and Wade Long. Special thanks to Peggy Grove and CHOICE Humanitarian/Salt Lake City, Utah.